ROGER L

ROMANO-BRITISH WALL PAINTING

SHIRE ARCHAEOLOGY

British Library Cataloguing in Publication Data
Ling, Roger
Romano-British wall painting.— (Shire archaeology; 42)
1. Mural painting and decoration, Roman— England
I. Title
751.7'3'09362 ND2575
ISBN 0-85263-715-2

Published by
SHIRE PUBLICATIONS LTD
Cromwell House, Church Street, Princes Risborough,
Aylesbury, Bucks HP17 9AJ, UK.

Series Editor: James Dyer

ISBN 0 85263 715 2

First published 1985

Set in 11 point Times and printed in Great Britain by
C. I. Thomas & Sons (Haverfordwest) Ltd,
Press Buildings, Merlins Bridge, Haverfordwest, Dyfed.

Contents

Acknowledgements

I am grateful to innumerable people for help, direct or indirect, in the preparation of this book — notably to the various excavators, museum curators and conservators who have given me access to material or who have provided photographs and drawings. They or their institutions are, I hope, fairly acknowledged in the captions to illustrations. Special thanks are due to my wife, who has read and criticised the text and has suffered vicariously from its birth pangs, besides enduring many long journeys to monuments and museums. Finally no book on Romano-British painting can ignore the debt of researchers to Dr Norman Davey; even where I have questioned aspects of his restorations, I remain acutely aware of his enormous contribution to the study of the subject. Without his work there would be precious little to write about.

List of illustrations

1
Introduction

Painted wall and ceiling plaster was one of the most widespread hallmarks of Roman civilisation. Throughout the Empire, whether in town or in country, in military or in civilian contexts, almost every building of moderate pretensions had plastered and painted walls, both inside and out — regardless of whether the walls were constructed of timber, of wattle and daub, of mud-brick, of mortared rubble or of stone. More often than not the plaster was merely whitewashed or painted in plain colours, for example red. Frequently the painting consisted of linear patterns on a white ground or of simple panel schemes in a restricted range of colours. But a surprisingly large number of interiors received quite elaborate polychrome murals including architectural elements, floral and vegetal motifs and human and animal figures. Such decorations were not confined to public buildings or grand mansions: one has only to visit Pompeii and Herculaneum to appreciate that even comparatively modest houses and shops had at least one or two finely painted rooms.

What was true of Pompeii and Herculaneum must also have been true of the towns and villas of Roman Britain. Almost every excavation in the lowland parts of the province, as well as many in the highland zones, yields fragments of painted plaster, sometimes in vast quantities. That so little, comparatively speaking, is known about Romano-British wall painting is due largely to the unfavourable conditions for its survival on most British sites. There have been no sudden burial and no deep protective blanket of volcanic ash to preserve the buildings; instead walls were left to weathering and progressive ruin (like many of the walls of Pompeii since they have been re-exposed) or were destroyed to make way for new buildings in medieval and modern times. Continuity of occupation in the towns of Roman Britain (*Verulamium* is one of the rare exceptions) has robbed us of much valuable evidence. Plaster is a fragile material and its position on walls and ceilings makes it peculiarly vulnerable: whereas a decorated pavement may be left undisturbed and sealed by silt or debris, wall and ceiling paintings are liable to be fragmented when the structure collapses. Worse, if a wall remains standing and exposed to the weather, the paintings may suffer bleaching and total disintegration. Thus the state of preservation of the

different media gives a completely false picture: there are far
fewer wall paintings surviving in Britain than there are mosaic
pavements, yet it is certain that the former were originally, as in
Pompeii, far commoner than the latter.

Until recently Romano-British wall painting was uncharted
territory. Occasionally a lucky chance had revealed parts of
standing walls with the plaster in position, as for example when
Samuel Lysons discovered the lower part of a figured mural at
Comb End in Gloucestershire in 1794 or when General Pitt-
Rivers unearthed a room with a panel decoration surviving to a
considerable height at Iwerne Minster in Dorset in 1897 (plate 9).
But there were no facilities and little incentive to try to preserve
such material in the eighteenth and nineteenth centuries and,
unless a drawing was made or a photograph taken, the discoveries
disappeared without trace. Most finds in any case took the form
of loose fragments and posed such daunting problems of salvage,
storage and reconstruction that few excavators were prepared to
do more than collect what they regarded as the more interesting
specimens. A signal exception was George Fox, who in 1896
carried out the first attempt to put together a painted pattern
from fragments; his experiment, involving material from a
rubbish heap at Silchester, may have led to false conclusions but
was nonetheless a commendable initiative, well ahead of its time.

The modern history of the study of Romano-British wall
plaster begins with the work of Lieutenant-Colonel G. W. Meates
and Mr C. D. P. Nicholson on plaster from the Roman villa at
Lullingstone in Kent. Here in the so called Deep Room,
discovered in 1949, thousands of fragments of paintings fallen
from an upper storey were collected and patiently put together by
Nicholson to form the well known series of Christian worshippers
(plate 1). The success of this work, which vividly (and unex-
pectedly) illustrated the potential value of wall plaster in
establishing the function of a room (the murals evidently came
from a house chapel) and in providing sociological information of
wider significance, pointed the way for future excavators. In the
1950s Professor Sheppard Frere's emergency work at *Verulamium* (near St Albans) revealed not just jumbled fragments but
broad sheets of plaster lying face down beneath overturned walls;
he called in Dr Norman Davey of the Building Research Station
at Garston, who was able to refine techniques for the lifting and
reconstruction of virtually complete decorative schemes, including the red wall and barley-stalk ceiling from House XXI.2 now
displayed in the Verulamium Museum (plate 16).

Plate 1. Fragments of the figure of an Orans (Christian at prayer) reconstructed by C. D. P. Nicholson from material excavated in the Lullingstone villa (Kent). Third quarter of fourth century. (Photograph: M. B. Cookson, by courtesy of G. W. Meates.)

It was no longer possible for excavators to ignore wall plaster, and the spate of rescue digs occasioned by urban development and motorway construction during the 1960s and 1970s provided an embarrassing mass of material. In some cases, as at Cirencester and Dover (figs. 2, 10), paintings were found still adhering to walls; but generally the archaeologist has been confronted with fallen fragments. Dr Davey, now working as a freelance restorer for the Inspectorate of Ancient Monuments, tackled a prodigious number of reconstructions, some of which, such as the figured murals from Kingscote (fig. 15), posed great difficulties. Although his techniques have aroused some controversy and many of his reconstructions are problematic, there is no doubt

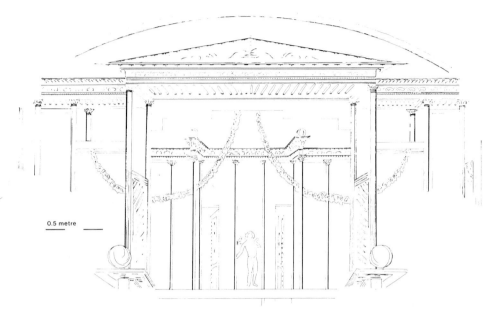

0.5 metre

Fig. 1. Reconstruction of the painted scheme from a lunette in a building at Southwark. Second century. (Drawing: S. A. Mackenna, by courtesy of the Department of Greater London Archaeology, Southwark and Lambeth.)

that without his work we would know far less today about Romano-British wall painting than we do. Others have followed in his footsteps. At Wimborne in Dorset Lieutenant-Colonel G. E. Gray has dedicated several years to assembling the tantalising remains of a superb set of figure paintings, as well as a painted vault, from a villa at Tarrant Hinton (plate 19); in the British Museum Miss Frances Weatherhead has done further important work on the huge Lullingstone jigsaw; and more recently Mr J. T. Sturge of the Leicestershire Museums has retrieved and pieced together the decorations on both faces of a wall which had collapsed into the cellar of a suburban villa at Leicester (plate 12, fig. 9). At the time of writing a well preserved architectural scheme from a possible bath house is being reconstructed at Southwark in London (fig. 1).

While this practical work has been going on, the late Miss Joan Liversidge collated and interpreted all the available material, whether newly excavated, rediscovered in museum basements or merely illustrated in old records. It is largely upon the foundations which she laid that the present writer was able to build the analytical commentary in his recent corpus *Wall Painting in Roman Britain,* published jointly with Dr Davey.

Plate 2. Lifting wall plaster at Boxmoor Roman villa, Hertfordshire. (Photograph: J. H. Brown, by courtesy of D. S. Neal.)

Plate 3a. Detail of a painted wall at *Glanum* (St Rémy-de-Provence) in 1957 (H. Rolland, *Gallia,* XVI (1958), page 112, fig. 12). (Photograph: A. Barbet.)
Plate 3b. The same detail in 1964. (Photograph: A. Barbet.)

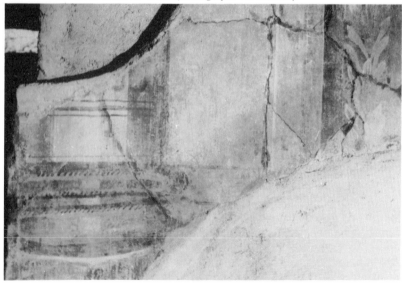

2
Excavation and restoration

The peculiar difficulties involved in the recovery and restoration of wall plaster require special comment before we can consider the general artistic and historical conclusions offered by the material.

If painted plaster is found in position on the walls, the problems of interpretation are less severe, because the decorative scheme (or at least a part of it) and the architectural context ought to be readily apparent; but the problem of conservation is acute. Ideally the paintings should be preserved and displayed *in situ;* indeed this is the only practicable policy at Pompeii and Herculaneum, where the volume of material is too great to be removed to museums and even the fallen fragments are replaced on the walls. This practice has the merit of allowing the public to appreciate the decorations in the original context but can only work in the long term if roofs are constructed and measures are taken to ensure a constant temperature and a constant level of humidity. The drawbacks of on-site conservation are all too clear at Pompeii and other Mediterranean sites, where the roofs have sometimes deteriorated or collapsed, leaving decorations exposed to the elements (plate 3), where vandals and graffitists are a persistent threat, and where thieves have occasionally broken in to cut out saleable pieces. As a result the authorities are faced with heavy recurrent costs both in respect of maintaining the fabric and in respect of policing, thus reducing the resources available for other work. In Britain the only monument where paintings have been preserved in this way is the so-called Painted House at Dover, and here an additional problem is caused by the leaching of salts from the walls, forming a white, potentially corrosive film over the surface.

In general there are only two sensible ways of dealing with paintings found in position. Either they can be drawn and photographed, then after any necessary consolidation reburied with sand or the like, in the hope that they will remain available for future generations; or they can be removed to a museum or depot. The second is the normal policy adopted where destruction is threatened or where practical considerations allow — and this not only in Britain but also in Italy, where the garden paintings from Livia's villa at Prima Porta have been transferred

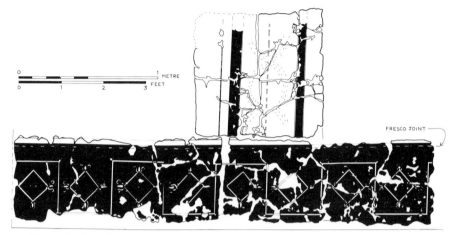

Fig. 2. Section of a wall decoration from Building XXIII.1 at Cirencester. Early second century. Corinium Museum, Cirencester. (Drawing: R. J. Ling, after A. Barbet.)

to the Terme Museum in Rome and two of the painted rooms from the House of the Griffins are now exhibited in the Palatine Antiquarium. If a decoration cannot be moved in its entirety, a sample may be taken, as with the piece from Building XXIII.1 at Cirencester now on display in the Corinium Museum (fig. 2).

Paintings surviving *in situ* are, however, the exception rather than the rule; normally, both in Britain and in other parts of the Empire, the excavator is confronted with fragments. Here different circumstances dictate different policies, but it is important to be aware of the options available and of the type of information that can be retrieved. Even deposits of plain white plaster have their value: they may yield evidence on technical processes and, if found lying undisturbed where they have fallen within the original building, they may give the approximate dimensions of the walls and the positions of doors, windows and niches. At the very least it is worth measuring the overall surface area of the fragments. With a painted decoration, it is necessary to keep all the fragments, including even the plain ones, until they have been thoroughly studied and if possible a reconstruction attempted. Generally, if the material is out of context or in a secondary context — shovelled into a rubbish pit, for example, or used as make-up in the foundations of a later building — its value is limited, though the presence of certain key elements may sometimes enable the pattern to be identified (see fig. 13). Much more important is the plaster found in a primary context, that is lying where it has fallen from the walls or ceiling. Here there is every chance that more or less complete decorations can be recovered. It is essential in such circumstances that careful and systematic recording should be carried out at the time of excavation, however slow and time-consuming the processes involved. Usually each layer in turn is carefully cleaned, drawn and photographed before removal, special note being taken of the distribution of the decorative elements where visible and of the way in which the fragments are lying (face up, face down, and so forth). The fragments are then collected and stored in boxes or trays labelled according to their layers and to their position within the room or excavation area (see fig. 3).

In due course the restorer must unpack the boxes in his workshop and begin the work of piecing the decoration together. In some cases large tracts can be reconstructed without difficulty from data gained in the field (joining areas are often fastened with plaster of Paris or an adhesive before lifting); in others, and particularly where for some reason methodical excavation was not possible, a gigantic jigsaw puzzle will result. This requires plenty of time and more especially plenty of space, since the whole assemblage needs to be laid out at once. All the familiar jigsaw techniques are employed — sorting according to colours or motifs, looking first for joins between the more distinctive pieces and then proceeding to the plainer pieces — but there are various

Fig. 3. Plan of fallen wall plaster at Sette Finestre, with areas labelled according to a storage system. (Drawing: R. J. Ling, after J. Liversidge, editor, *Roman Provincial Wall Painting of the Western Empire* (1982), fig. 1. 2.)

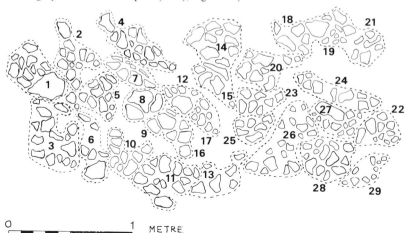

0   1   METRE

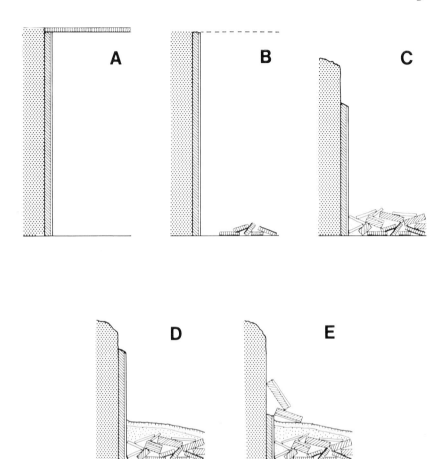

Fig. 4. Diagram of the collapse of wall plaster. (Drawing: R. J. Ling, adapted from A. Barbet.)

tell-tale indications other than those contained in the actual paintings. It helps, for example, to establish the orientation of fragments, which can be revealed in coarser work by the direction of brush strokes (which in single-colour fields and backgrounds tends to be vertical) and especially by drip marks. Surface blemishes and tool marks, the texture, thickness and structure of the plaster layers, and keying patterns on the reverse of the fragments are all additional aids to joining. It is important, therefore, not to remove any of the backing layers of the plaster at this stage; pieces of different thickness can be held in position by embedding them in trays of sand. With regard to keying patterns, that is the patterns transferred to the plaster in positive image from the pecking, roller imprinting or incising of the underlying surface, these too can assist with establishing the orientation: chevron patterns, for example, are invariably horizontal (plate 21). Even the size and condition of fragments can assist in the search for joins, since the smaller, more crumbly fragments may all have come from the same part of the wall, namely one which was particularly exposed or badly damaged, and the larger from a better protected zone such as the foot.

If the decoration is neither complete nor so nearly complete as to leave no doubt about its original form, the restorer's next task is to establish the relationship between the parts which he has reconstructed and to extrapolate from the known elements to the unknown. This is where a knowledge of the distribution of the fragments at the time of excavation becomes particularly useful. Pieces will obviously under normal circumstances have collapsed adjacent to the wall which they decorated, and, although in a small room there may be a certain amount of overlapping and intermixing, in most cases it is possible to assign the fragments to the appropriate walls. Moreover it can be assumed that their position along the wall corresponds roughly to their original place in the decoration. More difficulty is created by their varying levels and orientation; and here it is necessary to understand the stages in which the plaster is likely to have collapsed. Fig. 4 shows one possible course of events. It starts with the collapse of the ceiling plaster (B), followed by that of the upper part of the wall (C); the ceiling plaster generally, though not invariably, lies face downwards, but that from the wall may lie higgledy-piggledy, having sometimes slid down concertina-fashion. Of the remaining parts, the middle zone may have remained standing out of the rubble for a long period, exposed to weathering, and as a result entirely disintegrated (D) — hence the frequent difficulty in linking the upper and lower parts of a reconstructed mural (though this may also be due to the fracture of the wall). The plaster of the lower zone collapses last or, where buried, often remains in position (E); it is generally preserved in bigger pieces than the rest. The stratigraphy of a plaster deposit will therefore tend to be in an inverse relationship to the original position of the pieces on the wall, while the central parts may be missing altogether.

Being aware of this kind of sequence, and knowing the level at which the different pieces were found, the restorer will be better able to judge the role of his reconstructed elements in the decoration. He must also have a working knowledge of the general rules of Roman decorative composition, as demonstrated by well preserved examples elsewhere. Ceilings, where flat or vaulted, were decorated with all-over patterns based on squares, circles, octagons and the like, or with centrifugal designs arranged round a dominant central field; walls (plate 4) were almost invariably divided into three superimposed zones, namely the dado or socle, the central or main zone, and the upper zone or frieze, and within these the central zone, which was the widest and most elaborately decorated, was divided longitudinally into a number of fields taller than they were broad. Details of the treatment varied from period to period, but as a general rule corridors and long walls adopted an arrangement of repeating fields separated by narrow intervals or by imitation pilasters, while walls in normal-sized rooms were given a symmetrical scheme of either three or five fields, the decorative emphasis falling on the central one. The advantages of having this framework of reference are obvious. In ceiling patterns, if one or two elements are known, others can be restored in repeating sequence; on walls knowledge of details in one half may enable the restoration of corresponding details in the other, and a general familiarity with the colours and motifs used in different parts of the schemes will suggest where unplaced elements may be positioned. Finally it is possible to formulate certain rules of proportion which can assist us in gauging the size of a field or the height of a zone.

Unfortunately despite all these guides we can rarely do more than reconstruct small parts of a decoration, and large numbers, even the majority, of fragments remain unplaced. In this case it is useful to measure the total surface area of each colour or pattern to determine the relative proportions present, since this will give us at least some idea of the decorative emphasis.

Where a certain amount of reconstruction has been accomplished, the question arises of how it is to be mounted and displayed. Answers vary. The technique of Dr Davey involves mounting the plaster on aluminium mesh attached to wooden frameworks (plate 5), a method which has been criticised on the grounds that the resulting panels are excessively heavy and do not incorporate a sufficient degree of flexibility to allow for any expansion or contraction. Italian and French conservators on the other hand use a supporting structure in the form of a 'honeycomb' of cardboard coated with bakelite, which has the

Plate 4. Example of a typical wall decoration at Pompeii (colour lithograph published by W. Zahn, *Die schönsten Ornamente und merkwürdigsten Gemälde aus Pompeji, Herkulanum und Stabiae,* 1827-59).

advantage of being both lighter and more flexible (plate 6). A more radical difference of approach is in the treatment of missing areas. Dr Davey fills the spaces between genuine fragments with Polyfilla (a finely ground gypsum plaster with a cellulose filler) and paints in missing elements to match the ancient ones; but this has the danger of enshrining mistakes and giving the untrained observer a false sense of security. Moreover the Polyfilla sets so hard as to render corrections difficult: when a false conjunction was recognised in the Kingscote reconstruction, the ill fitting

Plate 5. Reconstructed plaster from Leicester mounted on aluminium mesh fixed to timber frames. (Photograph: Historic Buildings and Monuments Commission: Crown copyright reserved.)

areas had to be separated by the use of a saw. Other conservators refuse to mount fragments which do not join or whose position cannot be predicted with certainty; and the interspaces are filled with a mortar which is deliberately distinct in colour from the original plaster and is often set back to allow the latter to stand out in slight relief. If missing elements of the design can be supplied with a reasonable degree of confidence they are merely indicated in outline so that the museum visitor is under no misapprehension as to what is ancient and what is modern (plate

7). This method is preferable from both the scientific and the didactic viewpoints, and it will surely be the basis of the techniques used by future restorers: an excellent recent example is provided by Sturge's reconstruction of the two decorations from the suburban villa at Leicester.

Plate 6. Stages in the mounting of plaster at the Centre d'Étude des Peintures Murales Romaines in France: 1, fragment laid face downwards on gauze and canvas; 2, areas round fragment spread with synthetic mortar; 3, ancient mortar removed from rear of fragment; 4, second layer of synthetic mortar and gauze applied to create a level surface; 5, support ('honeycomb' sandwiched between layers of glass fibre impregnated with resin) attached to this surface. (Photograph: C. Allag, by courtesy of CNRS.)

Plate 7. Finished reconstruction of plaster from Genainville: Centre d'Étude des Peintures Murales Romaines. (Photograph: A. Barbet, by courtesy of CNRS.)

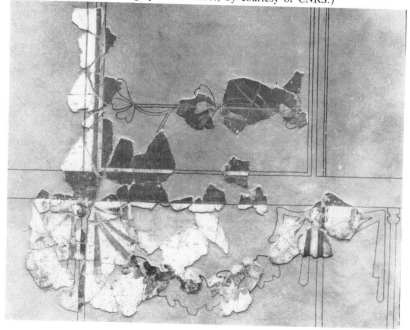

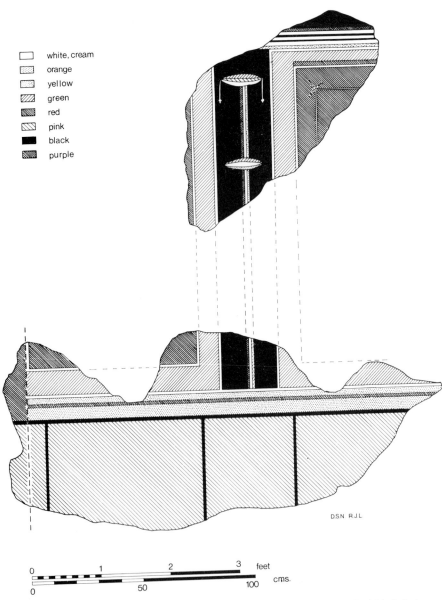

white, cream
orange
yellow
green
red
pink
black
purple

DSN RJL

0   1   2   3   feet
0   50   100   cms.

Fig. 5. Fragments of wall painting from the Flavian villa at Boxmoor (Hertfordshire). Late first century. (Drawing: R. J. Ling.)

3
Decorative schemes

Thanks to the work of the various restorers and researchers named in the previous pages, we are now able to review the decorative schemes employed by Romano-British painters. Regrettably, however, the dates available for many decorations are less precise than one would like: if we can date a building, it provides only the earliest limit for the plaster, which could have been added at a later period. The many examples of plasterwork which show two, three or even more successive painted surfaces demonstrate the frequency with which a room might be redecorated; at Catterick, for example, Davey was able to distinguish and partially reconstruct three separate phases of decoration from a building which was in use for little more than three quarters of a century. Conversely fragments of plaster found in destruction debris may be considerably earlier in time than any associated coins or pottery. Only when there is good evidence that the painting is a primary decoration or when it is closely confined between well dated phases of construction and destruction can we fix a date with greater precision. Perhaps the firmest indications are provided by the destruction levels left by Boudica's sack of *Verulamium*, Colchester and London, dated by the historian Tacitus to AD 61: since the standard of amenity reflected by wall paintings is not likely to have reached these cities till the mid or late 40s, fragments of painted plaster sealed by the Boudican layers, for example at *Verulamium*, can be dated within a span of ten years or so.

Given the problems of dating, it will be best to adopt an approach which is typological rather than chronological. We shall begin with wall decorations and look at ceilings afterwards.

Walls can be decorated in three principal manners: with simple panel schemes involving little or no illusion of depth, with architectural schemes which in some instances incorporate an element of perspective and illusionistic space, and with large-scale figure paintings which fill virtually the whole wall above the dado. Of these three types the first, the two-dimensional panel system, is by far the commonest (thus reflecting the situation in the neighbouring provinces) and occurs at all periods; it is the only form of wall decoration so far attested in Britain before the mid second century. Architectural schemes appear in the second half of the second and the early third century and still occur in the fourth century, though in a more stylised and pattern-like form. The open wall with figure paintings is a development restricted, as in Roman Italy, mainly to the third and fourth centuries.

The panel decorations known in Britain were divided, in the regular Roman manner already described, into a dado (from 1 to 3 feet, or 300 to 900 millimetres, in height), a panelled main zone roughly three times as high as the dado, and an upper zone, which is rarely preserved but which, where attested, seems to have been comparatively shallow and simply decorated — with horizontal stripes or vegetal motifs for example. The degree of richness was directly related to the choice of colour scheme. Most ornate, and largely confined to the first and second centuries, were polychrome decorations in which the dominant colours were yellow, red or green. Of the few known yellow schemes the most interesting are those of which tantalising traces were recovered in both the Neronian (about AD 60) and the Flavian (about AD 75) phases of the palace at Fishbourne (West Sussex); in one the yellow fields seem to have been separated by a vertical fascia with a fruit-laden candelabrum on a green background, and in another the fields contained an impressionistic landscape picture very reminiscent of painted landscapes of similar date in Rome and Pompeii (plate 8). Much more common, however, are red décors. The restored mural from a shop at Cirencester shows a simple version of a particularly popular scheme of Flavian or Trajanic times (69-117), in which the main zone consists of red fields set in a black surround, while the dado is pink with splashes of black, white, pale blue and red (a familiar technique designed to give the effect of marble veneer). Often, as here, the red fields have green or yellow borders edged with white lines and contain inner framing lines of yellow. Elsewhere the vertical black intervals between the fields were decorated with a candelabrum. A good example (fig. 5) has been discovered in a Flavian timber farm building at Boxmoor, near Hemel Hempstead, in which the dado was divided into long and short panels, again pink and stippled with black, white and purple spots, while the main zone contained red fields with green borders and intervening black fasciae bisected by a simple candelabrum with a white and purple stem interrupted by horizontal discs. Above ran a frieze of simple stripes suggestive of a moulded stucco cornice.

The general formula of red fields with green or yellow borders and black intervals carrying candelabra occurs repeatedly in late first-century and second-century decorations in France, Holland

Plate 8. Fragment of painted landscape from the Flavian villa at Fishbourne, (West Sussex) about AD 75. (Photograph: Sussex Archaeological Society.)

and Germany, though with greater elaboration in detail. One continental variant, the enrichment of the dado with clumps of reeds, a device which goes back to the so-called Fourth Style of painting in Italy, is attested in a few fragmentary schemes in Britain; but another, the insertion between the dado and the main zone of a predella containing plants, birds and animals, is so far unknown. Where elaboration occurs in British schemes, it takes the form of vari-coloured panelling in the dado and of foliate motifs in the main zone. Fragments of plaster from a building in the fort at Malton (fig. 6) suggest a decoration in which red fields slung with garlands alternated with black intervals carrying luxuriant vegetal candelabra, yellow with white side shoots and green leaves; the dado may have contained red lozenge-shaped panels set in pale blue rectangles, all on a yellow ground. While this example is probably datable to around the turn of the first and second centuries, still more elaborate but rather more formalised schemes can be dated to the second half of the second century. The best known examples are the red walls

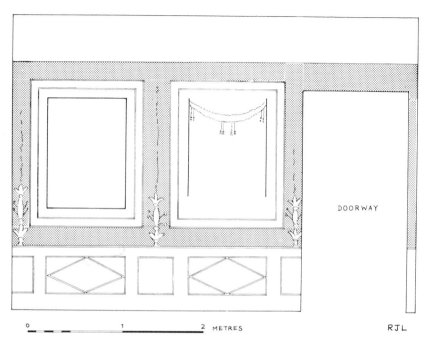

0   1   2 METRES   RJL

Fig. 6. Hypothetical reconstruction of a decorative scheme from the fort at Malton (North Yorkshire). Late first or early second century. (Drawing: R. J. Ling.)

from House XXI.2 at *Verulamium,* in which the main panels carried a central bird surrounded by a framework of delicate but stylised yellow candelabra and garlands, while the black surrounds were filled with formal arabesques. The dado consisted of alternate black and purple panels set on a yellow background. Remains of similar *de-luxe* decorations come from various sites, such as Colchester, Scampton (near Lincoln) and Winchester (where, however, the flowering shoots in the black intervals were apparently quite naturalistic: fig. 7).

Alongside red and black schemes there were also decorations in which a single ground colour ran right through the main zone, in panels and intervals alike; only the borders of the panels were carried out in a different colour. An early example, dated to the late first or early second century, comes from a house in Colchester. Above the usual pink dado with black splashes ran a series of pinkish-red fields framed by black borders between which vertical fasciae of the same pinkish-red colour carried elaborate vegetal candelabra in pink, white and cream. Fig. 8

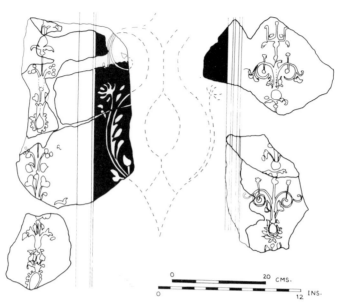

Fig. 7. Fragments of a red and black decoration from Winchester. The spacing of the fragments is arbitrary, and the broken lines are based on a similar motif in a decoration at *Verulamium*. Second century? (Drawing: R. J. Ling, adapted from A. Barbet.)

Fig. 8. Hypothetical reconstruction of a painted wall decoration from a house outside the west gate at Colchester (Balkerne Lane). Last quarter of first or early second century. (Drawing: R. J. Ling, with acknowledgements to Colchester Archaeological Trust.)

Plate 9. White-ground wall decoration in a villa at Iwerne Minster (Dorset), photographed in 1897. Fourth century. (Photograph: H. St George Gray, by courtesy of Dorset Natural History and Archaeological Society, Dorset County Museum, Dorchester, Dorset.)

shows a conjectural reconstruction of the scheme, which also included finely painted pictures of gladiatorial duels (see cover). Again at Colchester, but slightly later in date, probably belonging to the second quarter of the second century, are the remains of a decoration from a courtyard house outside the north gate; here, while the dado was treated in the more complex second-century manner with yellow panels 'floating' in a grey surround, the main zone was entirely red apart from green panel borders edged with the usual white lines. Such 'single-colour' decorative schemes were evidently popular in the south-east of the province during the second century because they were used in at least two rooms of House XXI.2 at *Verulamium* in the late Antonine period: on the end wall of corridor 3 the dominant colour was red, with panels outlined by yellow or purple, and in room 4 it was green, with panels framed in red. In both cases the dado seems to have been painted in imitation of marble veneering.

The simplest kind of panel decoration was a linear scheme on a white ground. This seems to have co-existed with more elaborate styles of decoration such as those already described, being used for subsidiary rooms and generally where a client wanted to spend less money. A typical example of such a white-ground scheme was the decoration at Iwerne Minster photographed by

H. St George Gray in 1897 (plate 9). Dated to the fourth century, this consisted of a dado flecked with pink and a main zone with fields outlined by lines and stripes of yellow, red and green; in the vertical fasciae which separated these fields were traces of green foliage. Remains of similar linear and striped panel systems are attested at *Verulamium* at all periods; and the three phases of decoration at Catterick, all probably datable to the second century, combined this treatment in the main zone with increasingly elaborate coloured dados. In one of the reconstructed murals from the suburban villa found at Leicester, datable to the late second or early third century, a main zone of fields framed by red, green and yellow bands is surmounted by a frieze containing a horizontal garland (fig. 9).

The second principal group of decorations are those with architectural schemes. A curious, and so far unique, compromise between two-dimensionality and illusionism is represented by the decoration of a corridor in House XXVIII.3 at *Verulamium,*

Fig. 9. White-ground wall decoration from a suburban villa at Leicester (Norfolk Street). Late second or early third century. Jewry Wall Museum, Leicester. (Drawing: R. J. Buckley, by courtesy of Leicestershire Museums, Art Galleries and Records Service.)

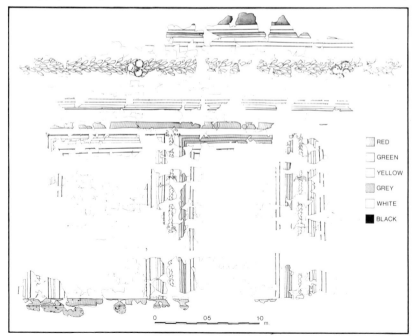

dated about AD 150 (plate 10). Here a basically two-dimensional
scheme of panels painted in imitation of exotic breccias and
alabasters is articulated with painted columns which have bases
characteristic of the western provinces and are rendered in full
trompe l'oeil with shading and highlights; yet, instead of being
shown in projection, standing on pedestals or on a podium, these
columns are apparently functionless, suspended in a purple
surround. More consistently illusionistic, though replete with
ornamental detail and employing architectural forms of a spindly
and unreal character, were the decorations from the colonnaded
court of a large town house in Leicester (Blue Boar Lane). Part of
the plaster of the west wall was found in position and showed a
'projecting' podium with a curving recess at the centre; but the
rest (or rather two sections of it) has had to be reconstructed from
fragments, with the result that many details are uncertain. The
general formula seems to have been an elaboration upon the red
and black schemes of *Verulamium* XXI.2, with which the present
decorations were perhaps roughly contemporary. The main
difference is that the black intervals were not simply treated as
fasciae with candelabra or arabesques but were opened up by
means of tall, slender columnar structures shown in perspectival
recession; these structures were apparently further enriched with
birds and flowering tendrils, while the dominant red fields
between them, adorned as at *Verulamium* with delicate yellow
and white candelabra and garlands, contained not birds but
human figures (sadly dehumanised and disfigured in the present
restoration). Above ran a series of rectangular panels with black
grounds containing theatrical masks (plate 11) and various
ornamental motifs. This evidently fine and ornate decoration
belonged to an eclectic style typical of Antonine decorations in
Roman Italy, where the scheme of the main zone can be roughly
paralleled at Ostia, though with a different combination of
colours (yellow and red rather than red and black). But the solid
podium is a feature which did not appear in the Ostian examples
and which is oddly at variance with the insubstantial structures
above: it smacks of the long outmoded Pompeian Second Style.
Another detail which was alien to contemporary Italian painting
was the series of ornamental panels along the top of the main
zone, a device which once again recalls the decorations of a much
earlier period, here the phase of transition between the Second
and Third Styles.

    The best examples of the architectural style in Britain are those
in the Painted House at Dover, where three adjacent rooms

Plate 10. Reconstructed wall painting with columns and panels of breccia and alabaster, from House XXVIII.3 at *Verulamium*. Mid second century. (Photograph: Verulamium Museum.)

Plate 11. Theatrical mask: detail of reconstructed wall painting from a town house at Leicester (Blue Boar Lane). Second century. (Photograph: Leicestershire Museums, Art Galleries and Records Service.)

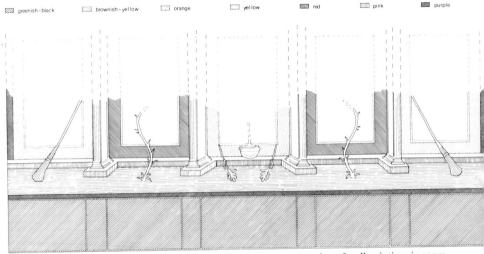

Fig. 10. Roman 'Painted House' at Dover: partial reconstruction of wall paintings in room 2 (not to scale). Second half of second or early third century. (Drawing: R. J. Ling.)

retain the lower parts of virtually identical decorations surviving to a height of nearly 2 metres (6 feet 7 inches) (fig. 10). In each case an illusionistic projecting podium whose front face is painted in imitation of veneering, either greenish-black or reddish-purple, supports a series of fluted columns shown as if engaged to pilasters or short spur walls; between the pilasters are panels with broad yellow, red or orange borders enclosing a white field; and in front of the panels are different motifs, such as a torch, a plant tendril (which actually grows from the podium), a leafy branch or palm frond, and a bowl with a plant. These paintings have been compared with the Second Style, with which they share the plasticity and realism of their architectural forms. But the Second Style had passed out of fashion in Italy in the late first century BC, while the Dover decoration belongs to the second half of the second century or to the early third century AD. Moreover there are certain features at Dover which are foreign to the Second Style: for instance the formula of a continuous podium supporting engaged columns and pilasters attached to a closed wall; the rhythmic alternation of the columns and the intervening panels (in the true Second Style columns are normally represented as free-standing and bisect the panels, which are conceived as passing behind them); the surrealist notion of a plant growing from the podium; the exceptionally high viewpoint from which the podium is seen; and the fact that the light radiates from a central source (in the true Second Style the light generally falls from one side, often in accordance with the real source of light in the room). The Dover paintings belong therefore to a renascence of the architectural manner, for which there are parallels in some decorations in Rome during the Antonine and Severan periods (AD 138-235).

During the third and fourth centuries architectural decorations continued in use, but with a lessening of the spatial factor and an increasing schematisation of details. The second of the reconstructed murals from the suburban villa at Leicester had a sequence of illusionistic Corinthian columns, each encircled by a spiralling vine scroll, and between them red and green fields, the former bedecked with naturalistic garlands, the latter with small framed pictures (plate 12). Despite the solidity of the columns, however, the podium was here reduced to a flat dado, and its 'upper surface' to a simple yellow band with the bases of the columns set on it, while the marble veneer of the 'front face' was rendered merely with an impressionistic play of streaks and blobs overlaid by scribbles. Later, in the second half of the fourth

Plate 12. Red and green wall from the Norfolk Street villa at Leicester. Late second or early third century. Jewry Wall Museum, Leicester. (Photograph: Leicestershire Museums, Art Galleries and Records Service.)

Plate 13. Head of a Cupid: detail of reconstructed paintings from Kingscote (Gloucestershire). Late third or early fourth century? Corinium Museum, Cirencester (in store). (Photograph: E. J. Swain, Kingscote Archaeological Association.)

century, the schematisation became much more pronounced. A decoration from the headquarters building of the fortress at York, though never so bizarre as in its present reconstruction, showed clear signs of the dissolution and stylisation of architectural form, most notably in the strong, harsh contours of the columns and in the disintegration of Corinthian capitals into amorphous clusters of leaves. Finally, in the Christian murals from Lullingstone (see plate 1), the worshippers floated within the intercolumniations of a fully pattern-like architectural framework carried out in garish and contrasting colours (blue, purple, pink, brown, yellow, orange etc). There was by now an almost total denial of volume and space.

Of the third main type of wall decoration, the large-scale all-over figured mural, there are few examples in Britain, and those which survive are mostly in a fragmentary state or have been unsatisfactorily reconstructed. One of the most spectacular, with figures over two-thirds lifesize, was excavated in 1976 in a building which formed part of a settlement near Kingscote in Gloucestershire. Areas reconstructed from fragments (see fig.

15) include the upper parts of two female figures with nimbed heads, a flying Cupid and two seated figures, one of which has a shield at its side, part of a reclining figure with a reed in the crook of its arm, and part of another figure next to a basket of flowers. Rendered predominantly in oranges, greens and purples on a white ground, these paintings show forms modelled in a fully classical style with assured, at times almost impressionistic, brush strokes (plate 13); whether they can be as late as the late third-century or fourth-century date proposed by the excavators is a matter for debate. The main theme represented has been identified as the love of Achilles and Deidameia (see further below).

Another mural with figures two-thirds life size, this time securely dated to the mid fourth century, was discovered in a mausoleum in the Poundbury cemetery outside Dorchester in Dorset (fig. 11). There were apparently serried ranks of standing figures along the south wall, if not round the whole interior. In the small fragment which has been reconstructed, the upper parts of four robed male figures are shown in conventional perspective, one row above the other, each man holding a knobbed staff.

Fig. 11. Reconstructed fragments of a figure frieze from a mausoleum in the Poundbury cemetery, near Dorchester (Dorset). Mid fourth century. (Drawing: R. J. Ling, with acknowledgements to Dorchester Excavation Committee.)

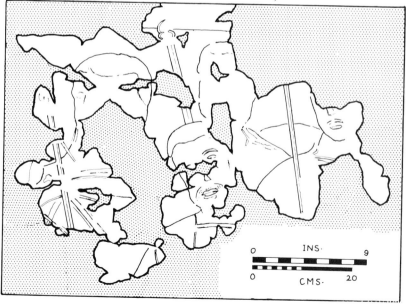

Fig. 12. Reconstruction of 'wallpaper patterns' from Silchester (Hampshire). Background reddish purple; pattern white, yellow, grey and green. Late second or early third century. (Drawing: R. J. Ling.)

What they represent is uncertain.

Tantalising fragments of large-scale mythological scenes, with almost lifesize figures against a turquoise background, have been reassembled by Lieutenant-Colonel Gray from the fragments at Tarrant Hinton. One area, which directly surmounts a pattern of imitation veneer, presumably part of a dado, shows the feet of a male figure standing with one foot resting on a block; the other includes the head of an effeminate youth, turned and tilted, with a spear or staff above one shoulder, and an apparently disembodied satyr's head attached to a rectangular block at the side (plate 19). The quality of these paintings is extremely fine and purely classical in style; like the Kingscote murals, they could possibly be earlier than the fourth-century date favoured by the excavators.

If the majority of wall decorations can be classified in the three categories which have been examined, a few minor genres stand apart. One is the garden painting at Fishbourne, an imitation shrubbery designed to appear as an extension of the real garden. Another is the so-called 'wallpaper pattern', in which the area above the dado was covered with an all-over network of ornament. In its simplest form this consisted merely of a lattice of intersecting lines, but more complicated versions could be based

Plate 14. Reconstruction by N. Davey of a coffered ceiling pattern from the villa at Gadebridge (Hertfordshire). The fragments used in the reconstruction were found dumped in a well. Second half of second century. Verulamium Museum (in store). (Photograph: Verulamium Museum.)

Fig. 13. Diagram showing position of original fragments in Gadebridge reconstruction. (Drawing: Y. Brown, by courtesy of Historic Buildings and Monuments Commission: Crown copyright reserved.)

Plate 15. Reconstruction by N. Davey of an octagonal ceiling pattern from the baths at Wroxeter (Shropshire). Second half of second or third century. (Photograph: Historic Buildings and Monuments Commission: Crown copyright reserved.)

on various combinations of brightly coloured medallions and floral motifs. These floral patterns have normally been ascribed to ceilings, but there are plenty of instances on the continent where they certainly belonged to walls, and the same must sometimes have been true in Britain: it is possible for example that at least one of the two patterns now reconstructed from Fox's Silchester fragments (fig. 12) may have derived from a wall and not, as formerly proposed, from a ceiling.

Ceilings can be more briefly reviewed. Here the general rule was all-over patterns based on recurring shapes: squares, octagons or medallions. In some instances the painter was clearly inspired by decorations in other media, notably stone and stucco relief, as in the coffer pattern reconstructed from fragments

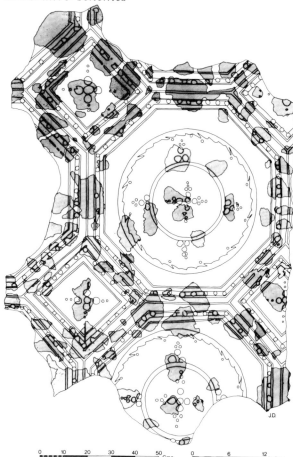

Fig. 14. Diagram showing position of original fragments in Wroxeter reconstruction. (Drawing: J. Dobie, by courtesy of Historic Buildings and Monuments Commission: Crown copyright reserved.)

found in the villa at Gadebridge (near Hemel Hempstead); here (plate 14; fig. 13) the pattern of squares containing rosettes, the framing cable enrichment, the predominant greyish-yellow colouring and the use of shading to give the effect of volume all indicate direct imitation of the carved coffering of Roman triumphal arches and of the moulded stuccowork of concrete vaults like those of the four-way arch beside the main street in Herculaneum. Similarly the reconstructed ceiling plaster from a bath suite in the villa of Dalton Parlours, near Collingham (West Yorkshire), employs greyish-yellow colouring and gradations of light and shade to produce an octagonal framework familiar in stuccowork. This same octagonal pattern can, however, be rendered in a more abstract, two-dimensional fashion, as in a

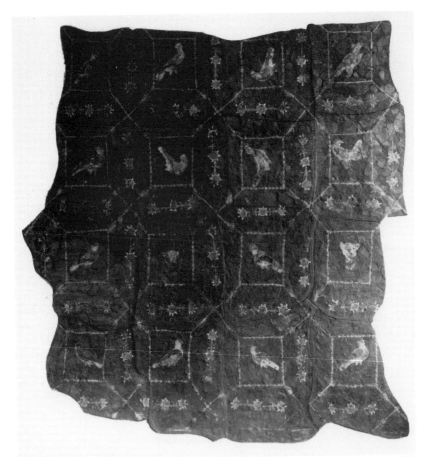

Plate 16. Reconstructed ceiling plaster from corridor 3 in*Verulamium* XXI.2, about AD 180. Verulamium Museum. (Photograph: M. B. Cookson, by courtesy of S. S. Frere.)

vault decoration from the baths at Wroxeter (Shropshire), carried out in lines and stripes of black and greyish-yellow on a white ground, with decorative enrichment in the form of clusters of black spots (plate 15; fig. 14). Of the purely ornamental ceiling patterns based on vegetal forms the best preserved is the ceiling from *Verulamium* XXI.2, in which a system of intersecting octagons was formed by yellow barley-stalks on a purple-red ground. The interstices were occupied by birds and panthers' heads, variously oriented to take account of the different positions which could be adopted by the viewers below (plate 16).

4
Iconography

As one might have expected with an art form which was brought to Britain as part of the Roman way of life, the subjects and motifs used in Romano-British wall painting were entirely derived from the repertory of the classical world. Conventional decorative motifs include the innumerable birds and vegetal motifs beloved of Roman art, as well as gorgon heads, theatrical masks and animal heads such as those in the *Verulamium* ceiling just described. Vegetal forms were especially popular, used both in a purely pattern-like manner, as in the *Verulamium* ceiling, and in more naturalistic styles, as in the hanging festoons of the red and green wall from the suburban villa at Leicester. A favourite motif, both in Britain and in Gaul, was a continuous plant scroll in the frieze above the main zone: of the examples which have been identified in Britain the best known is that of the yellow-ground frieze from*Verulamium* XXI.2 (now in the British Museum), in which the standard arrangement of side shoots spiralling alternately above and below a continuous undulating stem was accompanied, in the manner of the 'peopled scroll' of Roman sculpture, by the introduction of livestock — the same doves and panthers' heads as inhabited the ceiling of the neighbouring corridor (plate 17). Nor, in other contexts, were aquatic creatures neglected. A familiar theme in the decoration of bath suites was the aquarium, a loose aggregation of fish, polypods, crustaceans and the like swimming in a greenish-blue environment designed to suggest the sea. Such marine decorations are found in baths throughout the Empire, not only on painted walls and vaults but also (here generally with a white background) in mosaic pavements; and they must have been particularly appropriate in the context of plunge baths, like that of the so-called Forum Baths at Herculaneum, where the reflection of the painted aquarium in the real water would have given the bathers the impression that the fish were swimming amongst them.

Of special interest are figure subjects. Some, such as the gladiators from Colchester (front cover), betoken an interest in the entertainments of the Roman world — an interest which, in the case of the gladiators, was reflected by many later works of art and artefacts made in Britain, including the fourth-century mosaic at Bignor which showed Cupids in gladiatorial guise. A knowledge of Latin literature is revealed by fragments of painted scenes from a villa at Otford in Kent which would seem, from the accompanying inscriptions, to have been inspired by Virgil's *Aeneid*. Here, probably already in the first or second century, we have a foretaste of such later testimonies as the Dido and Aeneas mosaic from Low Ham in Somerset and the verse couplet on a mosaic at Lullingstone. Among religious themes, in addition to the Christian worshippers and the chi-rho monograms painted in the Lullingstone house chapel, we may include the three water nymphs of a much earlier mural in the Deep Room, also at Lullingstone. Their identity as nymphs is revealed by the overturned water vessel beneath the hand of one of them and by the spurts of water emerging from the breasts of another, a motif paralleled in a painting described by the third-century Greek writer Philostratus. What their role was at Lullingstone is uncertain, but their position on the back wall of a niche in a room which was otherwise decorated in a non-representational manner implies that they were the focus of some form of domestic cult. Perhaps they were the deities or spirits of a local stream.

More common than religious subjects or subjects drawn from Roman life and literature are the general themes of classical mythology. It is unfortunate that most of the more elaborate mythological scenes to have survived are woefully fragmentary and incomplete or have been restored in such a manner as to obscure their meaning. A few of the more interesting examples may be mentioned. At Southwell (Nottinghamshire) a finely painted Cupid was shown flying or swimming, perhaps in the company of one or more sea nymphs, in a marine environment (plate 18). Although the mixing of a winged creature with the denizens of the deep might seem an odd conjunction, it is paralleled in Roman mosaics and sarcophagus reliefs; while some show Cupids riding dolphins, others show them actually swimming. From Tarrant Hinton (Dorset) come the intriguing fragments of figure scenes already described. For the figure standing with one foot on a block it is impossible to suggest any firm identification, though the posture is known from various Roman paintings, such as those of Perseus rescuing Andromeda and of Argos guarding Io which were probably based on works by the classical Athenian master Nicias. In the other scene (plate 19) the effeminate face of the principal figure, the angle of his head and shoulder, and the presence of a spear or staff all bring to mind the characteristic iconography of Narcissus, who was

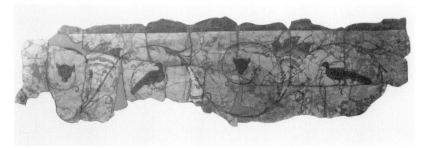

Plate 17. Yellow frieze with 'peopled scroll' from *Verulamium* XXI.2, about AD 180. British Museum. (Photograph: M. B. Cookson, by courtesy of S. S. Frere.)

Plate 18. Cupid in a marine enviroment, from the villa at Southwell (Nottinghamshire). Late second or early third century. Southwell Minster. (Photograph: Historic Buildings and Monuments Commission: Crown copyright reserved.)

Plate 19. Fragments of a wall painting (Narcissus at the spring, or the Judgement of Paris?) from a villa at Tarrant Hinton (Dorset). Early fourth century? Priest's House Museum, Wimborne (in store). (Photograph: A. G. Giles.)

frequently shown seated, his weight supported on one arm, his head languidly tilted to catch the reflection of his face in the pool below, and his hunting spear or spears resting against his arm or shoulder. If the painting did indeed depict Narcissus, the block at the right may have been a stone fountain, the source of the water, and the satyr's head may have been a carved waterspout. Alternative explanations of the scene are, however, not excluded. Many fragments remain unplaced, including some with further parts of staffs or spears, one of which has a trumpet-shaped mouth or terminal. Future reconstruction may put a different complexion on the problem.

The figure scene which has excited the greatest controversy is that from Kingscote (Gloucestershire; fig. 15). The presence of a Cupid and of a figure with a shield at its side implies a myth containing a love element and involving a martial deity or hero. At the same time the figure with the shield wears the long drapery of a female but exposes the left leg in a manner which would be unseemly in a martial goddess such as Minerva. It is argued, therefore, that the scene showed Achilles disguised as a woman on Skyros, where his mother Thetis had hidden him to prevent his premature death at the siege of Troy. The female figures with nimbed heads might therefore be the daughters of Lycomedes, the king of Skyros; the Cupid would symbolise the love between Achilles and one of the daughters, Deidameia; and the shield would be part of the weaponry brought by the Greeks Odysseus and Diomedes to lure Achilles into revealing himself. It appears that the hero has been given his armour but lingers a moment on his throne, as though reluctant to be carried to war.

Fig. 15. Central group of Kingscote figure painting, restored from fragments. The stippled areas are modern plaster. Late third or early fourth century? (Drawing: A. Barbet, H. Eristov and R. J. Ling, with acknowledgements to Corinium Museum, Cirencester.)

0   50   100   cms.

There are, however, a number of features which are out of keeping with the court of Lycomedes. In particular it is odd that the daughters should wear nimbi, the attributes of deities or personifications rather than mere mortals. Besides, the hero's seat seems too low to have been a chair or throne and rather suggests an open-air setting. Possibly therefore the figure was not Achilles but Venus posing with the shield of her consort Mars, a subject familiar in Roman art. In this case the attendance of Cupid, Venus's son, would be particularly apt, and the theme of the wall decoration would tally with that of the mosaic pavement in the same room, which contained a bust of Venus in the central position. The whole question of interpretation must remain open.

5
Social and artistic context

The subject matter of the paintings is not only of intrinsic interest but also a valuable index of the patron's culture and tastes. Each wall decoration was a special commission, carried out on the spot and unique to the room in which it was applied: the painters had pattern books which they would show their clients, much like the modern purveyors of wallpaper, but the fact that their work was created spontaneously within its intended setting inevitably encouraged improvisation and probably allowed the patron a considerable measure of control over the choice and arrangement of motifs. It is difficult to believe that elements such as the Colchester gladiators or the Otford Virgilian scenes would have been admitted without the patron's active interest and approval, and even more so with religious themes such as the worshippers and Christian symbols of the Lullingstone chapel, which can only have been a special commission.

The general distribution and location of painted decorations in the province is also of some sociological interest. Totally unknown in Celtic society, wall paintings were quick to appear as one of the marks of Romanisation after the conquest and were a well established domestic amenity in the major towns of the south-east, such as London, Colchester and *Verulamium,* as well as in the grand Mediterranean-style villa at Fishbourne (West Sussex), by the time of Nero (AD 54-68). By the second century there were wall paintings throughout the province, in towns and villas alike; only in the outlying and upland regions, where a traditional iron age lifestyle remained the rule, did their distribution become thinner. Painted plaster was now an essential part of civilised living — much more so than mosaic pavements, which were an altogether rarer phenomenon, confined to odd rooms in the especially well-to-do residences.

Not all wall paintings were equally elaborate and expensive. As we have seen, rich polychrome decorations and comparatively simple schemes existed side by side, often in the same house: the finer paintings were reserved for the more important rooms, such as dining and reception rooms, colonnaded courts, bath suites and the chief bedchamber, while the simpler were relegated to the subsidiary rooms and areas, for example the minor bedrooms and service quarters. Thus in the house in Blue Boar Lane at

Leicester the ornate red and black decorations of the court contrasted with somewhat simpler paintings in some of the rooms which opened off it. Frequently, as in the fourth-century villas at Rudston (Humberside) and Sparsholt (Hampshire), the finest wall decoration occurred in the room with the most elaborate, or indeed the only, mosaic pavement; and this room might be further singled out, as in the villa at Brantingham (Humberside) and in a house in the civilian settlement at Malton (North Yorkshire), by being provided with underfloor heating. In more modest houses, such as the Flavian timber villa at Boxmoor (Hertfordshire) and the fourth-century farmhouse at Iwerne Minster (Dorset), only one room seems to have received a painted decoration. There is little doubt that such rooms were the 'best' rooms, those in which guests would be entertained, and that wall paintings were to some extent a status symbol. They were also a moderately expensive amenity, especially in their more richly coloured and elaborately detailed forms, since otherwise it would have been unnecessary to grade the rooms. The fact that mosaic pavements were used more sparingly than paintings indicates that commissioning a mosaic was even more costly — evidently not because the mosaicist was paid more than the painter (we have documentary evidence from the early fourth century that the reverse was true) but because of the time that it took and the cost of the materials involved.

How was the wall-painting 'industry' organised to meet the demand? This is a difficult question to answer, given the fragmentary and defective nature of the evidence; but the ubiquity of wall paintings in the lowland zones and the frequency with which such paintings were renewed combine with analogy from Pompeii and other Mediterranean sites to suggest that there was at least one workshop, if not more, in every fair-sized town. Rural sites would have been served from the nearest towns; thus, for example, the painters who worked in the Humberside villas at Brantingham and Winterton may have come from Brough on Humber *(Petuaria)*. A similar kind of organisation can be discerned in the distribution of mosaics, where the evidence is more complete and better preserved, and where important researches by Dr David Smith of Newcastle University have identified groupings of common patterns and motifs in different parts of the province. Although the picture is doubtless complicated by such factors as branch workshops, itinerant craftsmen and simple plagiarism, there is no reason to doubt Smith's general conclusion that there were broadly regional 'schools' focused on centres such as Colchester or *Verulamium* (or London?) in the second century and Cirencester, Dorchester (Dorset), Brough on Humber and somewhere in the East Midlands, possibly Water Newton *(Durobrivae)*, in the fourth century. It is probable, in view of the greater demand for paintings, that painters' workshops were more numerous and therefore that painters had to travel less far to find commissions than mosaicists did; but even so there are hints of regional motifs prevalent in certain broad sectors of the province. Lozenge-shaped panels in a 'marbled' dado seem to have been especially popular in Yorkshire and Humberside; decorative spots applied in a dark colour over a light-coloured band are found in paintings along the Severn valley from Shropshire (plate 15) and Hereford and Worcester down to Gloucestershire and Gwent; and the curious device, almost unparalleled outside Britain, of painted patterns designed to imitate mosaic, tesserae and all, is attested from sites in the south and west (West Sussex, Hampshire, Gloucestershire and Somerset). In each area we can postulate the existence of interrelated workshops based in the main towns of the region. This represents the situation in the later centuries of the Roman period. Initially, when wall painting was a new craft in the province, the practitioners must have followed the Roman armies, officials and merchants from the continent; and it is striking that some of the earliest representational paintings, such as the Fishbourne landscape and the Colchester gladiators, are particularly firmly embedded in the classical tradition and vie in quality with the best work from Mediterranean sites. It was these immigrant painters who must have trained local apprentices and thus founded the network of workshops that served the province from the second century onwards.

Wall paintings did not appear in isolation: they formed part of a decorative ensemble which included work in mosaic and in other media (stuccowork, marble veneer), and they were also intended to be seen in a specific architectural setting. These aspects, however, are difficult to appreciate from the British evidence. In a few isolated cases, some of which have been mentioned (Malton, Rudston and Brantingham, for example), we know that polychrome murals were combined with an elaborate figured mosaic pavement; but in others, following a rule which seems to have prevailed in Roman Italy during the late Republican and early Imperial periods, decorators preferred to offset richly painted walls with simple floor decorations, either in *opus signinum* (mortar containing powdered brick) or in plain

tessellation. The murals in the Painted House at Dover, for
example, were associated with *opus signinum* pavements, and the
red walls from the corridor in *Verulamium* XXI.2 with tessellation. In the latter case, however, the tessellation was of brick,
and the conjunction of a red floor with predominantly red walls
and a purple-red ceiling (the 'barley-stalk' plaster) must have
produced a somewhat overwhelming ensemble. The neighbouring dining room, in which the famous lion mosaic, with its
predominantly white and red tones and its broad red border, was
combined with a green wall, must have been less oppressive but
still rather garish. Such décors offer an interesting comment on
the taste of the householders; but they were probably the
exception rather than the rule. Normally an effort was made to
achieve a pleasing colour balance: for ceilings in particular a
white ground seems to have been favoured in most cases, thus
offering a foil to the polychromy of walls. And that some thought
went into the relationship of floor, walls and ceiling is implied by
the occasional use of common subjects or motifs. At Brantingham, for instance, the busts of nimbed female figures in the
mosaic pavement were evidently matched by similar busts
painted on the walls or ceiling; at Kingscote, as we have seen, the
theme of the mosaic pavement, the goddess Venus, may have
been picked up on at least one of the walls; and in the
Verulamium corridor the walls and ceilings were linked by their
common use of birds as a decorative motif.

On the relationship of painted decorations to their architectural context we can say almost nothing (beyond what has already
been said about the relation between the richness of a decoration
and a room's function). However, the scale of the component
parts would vary according to the size of a room: that is, the
height of the zones would be adapted according to the height, and
the width of the main panels according to the length, of the walls.
This can to some extent be confirmed where decorations are well
preserved. In the Painted House at Dover, for instance, each of
the preserved murals was divided into an exact number of panels,
five on the long walls and three on the shorter ones, always with
centralised perspective. But, as invariably at Pompeii, the spacing
and perspective were planned with little reference to the
doorways, which were allowed to cut across panels almost
indiscriminately. Irregularities in the shape of a vault or ceiling
must also frequently have forced the painter into compromises,
especially where he was using a radiating design which required a
square surface; all-over patterns, however, had the advantage of

being highly adaptable, for if the available surface was trapezoidal rather than rectangular they could simply be run on till they met the edge. Unfortunately no British ceiling decoration is well enough preserved to show how painters faced these problems in practice.

Plate 20. Detail of wall plaster in the suburban villa at Leicester (Norfolk Street) showing 'pecking' for a new decoration. (Photograph: Leicestershire Museums, Art Galleries and Records Service.)

6
Techniques of plasterers and painters

The technical aspects of Roman wall paintings can be studied from the surviving remains and to some extent from the literary evidence. There were two main stages: the application of the plaster and the application of the paint.

In plastering the first step was to ensure good adherence to the underlying surface. Where this surface was rough or absorbent, as was the case with brickwork, most types of stonework and the reeds normally used for suspended ceilings, there was no need to take special measures; but on smooth surfaces some form of key had to be prepared. The main evidence comes from daub or cob walls, which were scored or imprinted, while still soft, with criss-cross or zig-zag patterns: an excellent example of a wattle and daub wall from Colchester, now reconstructed in the Colchester and Essex Museum, carries bands of lozenges evidently applied with stamps or rollers. Where an underlying surface was hard or dry, however, and particularly when a new layer of plaster was to be applied over a pre-existing decoration, a key was prepared by pecking the surface with a pick-hammer or similar implement (plate 20). The signs of this process, as of the more common zig-zag keying, are frequently visible in relief on the reverse of plaster fragments (plate 21).

The plaster itself was built up in a number of layers. These were based on slaked lime (calcium hydroxide), which in the process of 'setting' gives off water vapour and takes up carbon dioxide from the air to form calcium carbonate; but their colour and texture varied according to the gritty material added to give them body. In the underlying layers this was normally sand, incorporated in the ratio of two or three to one (as in bonding mortar) while in the finishing layer, where a fine white appearance was desired, it was frequently some form of powdered calcite or (ideally) marble flour. The architectural writer Vitruvius recommends, in addition to a render coat, no less than six layers of wall plaster, three incorporating sand, and three marble flour, but this ideal was rarely attained in Britain, where there were at most two coats of sand 'mortar' and one finer white surface layer. As to the precise nature and sources of the ingredients used, no reliable petrological analyses have been carried out on the British material as they have in France and

Plate 21. Fallen sheet of wall plaster at *Verulamium* (House XXI.2) showing imprints of zigzag keying patterns from a daub wall. (Photograph: E. Birchenough, by courtesy of S. S. Frere.)

Plate 22. Detail of painting at Kingscote (Gloucestershire), showing evidence of fresco technique. (Photograph: N. Davey.)

Italy. Sometimes, however, a distinctive aggregate can be plausibly identified by eye, such as the local red sand of the Chester area; and a frequent and unmistakable component is pulverised brick, used in damp conditions to make the plaster waterproof.

Each layer was applied, as Vitruvius tells us, before its predecessor was entirely dry, so that the moisture was initially drawn inwards and the whole cohered to form a compact mass. Ultimately, when the finishing coat had been spread, the moisture would begin to rise to the surface and then to evaporate; and this was the stage at which the painter began work.

There is little doubt that the ground colours of Roman murals, and probably much of the detailed patternwork and figure painting, were carried out in the fresco technique: in other words the pigments were applied while the plaster was still damp and were subsequently fixed by the chemical reaction as the evaporating water brought lime to the surface, forming a transparent film of calcium carbonate over them. Vitruvius clearly describes a fresco process (even though he did not understand how it worked), and there are surviving paintings, those from Kingscote for example, which show how the painter's brush strokes smoothed out or furrowed the soft plaster (plate 22). In the expensive polychrome decorations the surface was burnished with stone rubbers or floats after the ground colours had been spread, thus producing the characteristic sheen of Roman frescoes. Painted detail added over the ground colours could then have been applied in tempera, that is with an organic binding medium such as size, or in *fresco secco,* a technique in which the pigments are applied to a dry ground but mixed with limewater in order to achieve the fixing reaction of true fresco. Even at this stage the original plaster may have retained sufficient moisture for such expedients to be unnecessary. Examination of Pompeian paintings under raking light has revealed that figures on coloured surfaces were frequently burnished into the background, producing slightly sunken areas and a slightly darker colouring in the immediate vicinity; the plaster must therefore still have been soft and a true fresco process still operable.

One of the characteristic features of fresco painting is the division of the wall into *giornate di lavoro* — areas which could be conveniently handled by the artist while the plaster retained an ideal level of dampness. The seams which mark the joining of such areas are clearly discernible on many Roman murals, usually running horizontally between the three zones of the decorative scheme but sometimes, if the wall was ·long or the decoration particularly complex, forming vertical divisions as well (fig. 16). In Britain the clearest evidence comes from the suburban villa at Leicester, where joints in the red and green mural can be distinguished along the top and bottom of the main zone and also vertically at the edges of two of the columns. Making these joints coincide with lines in the decorative scheme was a matter of convenience for the painter but it had the additional advantage of helping to mask the transitions once the work was complete. For details which required special care, notably any framed mythological picture within the wall, fresh plaster would often be applied, even at the expense of chipping away the surface which had already been laid.

The pigments available to the painter were chiefly earth colours — red ochre, yellow ochre, green earth *(terre verte)* and chalk-based white. Black was obtained from soot or charcoal, and blue from an artificially produced glassy pigment commonly known as 'blue frit' or 'Egyptian blue'. Vitruvius and the elder Pliny, who wrote a book on natural science in the first century AD, give long lists of pigments, which Pliny divides into 'plain' and 'florid', the former evidently held in stock by painters, the latter to be supplied by the patron; but the analyses so far carried out in Britain, as in other parts of the Empire, reveal that for the

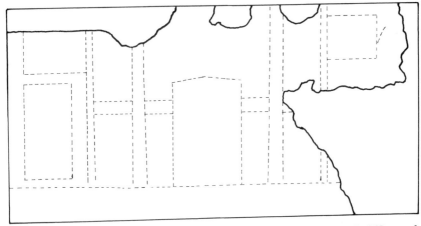

Fig. 16. Diagram showing *giornate di lavoro* in a frescoed wall in the so-called House of Livia in Rome. The joints are indicated by broken lines. Finer plaster was used for the panel pictures and architectural perspectives than for the plainer areas of the painting. (Drawing: R. J. Ling, after *Bollettino d'arte*, XXXIV (1949), page 149, fig. 8.)

vast majority of commissions only a restricted range of basic pigments was used. Of the 'florid' pigments some, such as Tyrian purple, would not have survived anyway; but others, such as cinnabar (bright red mercuric sulphide), can be identified with little difficulty, yet are rarely found. Cinnabar itself, known from a number of *de luxe* decorations in Rome and Pompeii, has been positively confirmed on plaster fragments from only four British sites, York, Leicester, London (the plaster at Southwark) and the villa at Piddington (Northamptonshire), though it may be suspected in some other instances where analysis has not been attempted. Its costliness is amply indicated by Pliny, who gives the price as 50 sesterces a pound, as against 2 *denarii* (8 sesterces) for the best red ochre, which came from Sinope on the Black Sea, and 8 *asses* (2 sesterces) for red from Africa. Only the most affluent patrons would have paid this sort of price. Apart from cinnabar and blue frit, all of the pigments identified in Britain could have been obtained from native sources and would thus have been comparatively cheap. But one material which was certainly expensive was gold leaf, employed occasionally in Britain and in other parts of the Roman world to enhance selected details in both painting and stucco relief. Fragments of plaster with traces of gilding, probably fixed with some organic medium, are now known from three British sites: Colchester, Lincoln and London (Southwark again).

The painter's tools were few and modest. In grinding and mixing the colours, and in applying them to the wall, he would have used much the same equipment as his successors in medieval times and ever since — mortars and pestles, paint pots, palettes (often apparently furnished by oyster shells), brushes of pigs' bristles or of finer hair. For the general layout of his scheme he would have needed a chalkline, rules and compasses, and in addition some form of pointed implement to score or impress the basic guidelines in the plaster. The purpose of these guidelines was merely to ensure that accurate alignments and regular spacing were maintained, and they were sparingly employed; all the more so were the preliminary sketches for figure paintings, incised with a burin.

What is chiefly remarkable about the whole painting process is the degree of freedom with which the ancient wall painter worked. Though pattern books were used and there are striking similarities between decorative motifs and figure compositions in far-flung regions of the Empire, no two decorations are identical. Even among the hundreds of wall paintings known from Pompeii the degree of repetition is extraordinarily small, being confined in each case to the odd figure subject or to a handful of ornamental motifs. Decorators seem to have aimed to ring the changes in every new project which they undertook; and it is symptomatic of their attitude that, when repetition does occur, the motif in question is often used in a different way or in a different position. Moreover, almost no element is carried out in a mechanical manner: even the most repetitive ornament, however finicky it was to produce, would invariably be painted freehand. And all this would have been done time and time again in the living quarters of private houses, whether grand or comparatively modest — in the context where today's householder would be content with a plain coat of paint or with a mass-produced wallpaper. It is these factors of spontaneity and universal availability that give Roman wall painting its unique appeal and its exceptional social interest.

7
Further reading

Davey, N., and Ling, R. J. *Wall Painting in Roman Britain.*
Britannia Monograph Series 3. Society for the Promotion of
Roman Studies, 1982. The fullest and most up-to-date survey
of the evidence.

Other general discussions
Davey, N. 'The Conservation of Romano-British Painted Plas-
ter.' *Britannia* 3 (1972), 251-68.
Liversidge, J. 'Wall Painting in Roman Britain: A Survey of the
Evidence.' *Antiquity and Survival* 2 (1957-8), 373-86.
Liversidge, J. *Britain in the Roman Empire.* Routledge and
Kegan Paul, 1968. Pages 84-98.
Liversidge, J. 'Furniture and Interior Decoration' in Rivet, A. L.
F. (editor), *The Roman Villa in Britain.* Routledge and Kegan
Paul, 1969. Pages 127-72.
Liversidge, J. 'Recent Developments in Romano-British Wall
Painting' in Munby, J., and Henig, M. (editors), *Roman Life
and Art in Britain.* British Archaeological Reports 41, 1977.
Pages 75-103.
Toynbee, J. M. C. *Art in Roman Britain.* Phaidon Press, 1962.
Pages 193-6, plates 195-205.
Toynbee, J. M. C. *Art in Britain under the Romans.* Oxford
University Press, 1964. Pages 213-27.

Individual sites
Boon, G. C. *Silchester: The Roman Town of Calleva.* David and
Charles, 1974. Pages 211-3.
Crummy, P. *Excavations at Lion Walk, Balkerne Lane, and
Middleborough, Colchester, Essex.* Colchester Archaeological
Report 3. Colchester Archaeological Trust, 1984. Pages 42,
146-53, 180-2.
Cunliffe, B. W. *Excavations at Fishbourne 1961-1969.* Reports of
the Research Committee of the Society of Antiquaries of
London, XXVI (1971), II, 50-82.
Frere, S. S. 'Excavations at *Verulamium* 1956: Second Interim
Report.' *Antiquaries Journal* 37 (1957), 1-15.
Frere, S. S. 'Excavations at *Verulamium* 1958: Fourth Interim
Report.' *Antiquaries Journal* 39 (1959), 1-18.

Frere, S. S. *Verulamium Excavations,* II. Reports of the Research Committee of the Society of Antiquaries of London, XLI (1983). Pages 162-7, 239.

Gray, G. E. 'Romano-British Wall Paintings from Tarrant Hinton, Dorset' in Liversidge, J. (editor), *Roman Provincial Wall Painting of the Western Empire.* British Archaeological Reports International Series 140, 1982. Pages 145-52.

Ling, R. J. 'Two Silchester Wall-Decorations recovered.' *Antiquaries Journal* 64 (1984).

Liversidge, J. 'Wall Paintings from Verulamium.' *British Museum Quarterly* 25 (1971), 87-93.

Liversidge, J. 'The Wall-Paintings' in Liversidge, J., Smith, D. J., and Stead, I. M., 'Brantingham Roman Villa; Discoveries in 1962.' *Britannia* 4 (1973), 99-103.

Liversidge, J. 'Winterton Wall-Painting' in Stead, I. M., *Excavations at Winterton Roman Villa.* HMSO, 1976. Pages 272-87.

Liversidge, J. 'Wall-Paintings' in Stead, I. M., *Rudston Roman Villa.* Yorkshire Archaeological Society, 1980. Pages 139-45.

Meates, G. W. *Lullingstone Roman Villa.* Heinemann, 1955. Pages 126-42.

Meates, G. W. *Lullingstone Roman Villa.* Ministry of Works guide book, HMSO, 1962. Pages 31-3, 37 f.

Mellor, J. E. 'New Discoveries from the Norfolk Street Villa, Leicester' in Liversidge, J. (editor), *Roman Provincial Wall Painting of the Western Empire.* British Archaeological Reports International Series 140, 1982. Pages 127-40.

Philp, B. J. *The Roman Painted House at Dover.* Kent Archaeological Rescue Unit, no date (1977?).

Sturge, J. T. 'The Lifting of the Roman Wallplaster from the Norfolk Street Roman Villa, Leicester, England' in Liversidge, J. (editor), *Roman Provincial Wall Painting of the Western Empire.* British Archaeological Reports International Series 140, 1982. Pages 141-4.

Swain, E. J. and Ling, R. J. 'The Kingscote Wall-Painting.' *Britannia* 12 (1981), 167-75.

Weatherhead, F. J. 'The Restoration of the the Lullingstone Roman Wall-Plaster' in Liversidge, J. (editor), *Roman Provincial Wall Painting of the Western Empire.* British Archaeological Reports International Series 140, 1982. Pages 153-9.

8
Monuments and museums to visit

The following museums, according to the latest information, have interesting pieces of plaster. Intending visitors are advised to telephone the museum before making a special journey, to find out the opening times and to confirm that the relevant items are on display.

Bignor Roman Villa, Bignor, Pulborough, West Sussex RH20 1PH. Telephone: Sutton, West Sussex (079 87) 259. Roman villa, site museum. Reconstructed panel (contentious) of imitation veneer.

Birmingham Museum and Art Gallery, Chamberlain Square, Birmingham B3 3DH. Telephone: 021-235 2834. Fragments from Droitwich.

Brading Roman Villa, Brading, Sandown, Isle of Wight. Telephone: Isle of Wight (0983) 406223. Roman villa, site museum. Fragment with bowl of fruit.

British Museum, Great Russell Street, London WC1B 3DG. Telephone: 01-636 1555 or 1558. Reconstructions from Lullingstone and *Verulamium.*

Cambridge University Museum of Archaeology and Anthropology, Downing Street, Cambridge CB2 3DZ. Telephone: Cambridge (0223) 359714. Fragments from Cambridgeshire villas, including Ickleton.

Colchester and Essex Museum, The Castle, Colchester, Essex CO1 1TJ. Telephone: Colchester (0206) 576071 or 574363. Fragments from various sites, including the gladiator from Balkerne Lane.

Corinium Museum, Park Street, Cirencester, Gloucestershire GL7 2BX. Telephone: Cirencester (0285) 5611. Reconstructed parts of panel decorations. Further material in store, including Kingscote reconstructions.

Fishbourne Roman Palace, Salthill Road, Fishbourne, Chichester, West Sussex PO19 3QR. Telephone: Chichester (0243) 785859. Roman palace and site museum. Fragments, including part of a landscape panel.

Hull Transport and Archaeology Museum, 36 High Street, Kingston upon Hull, North Humberside HU1 1NQ. Tele-

Romano-British Wall Painting

phone: Hull (0482) 222737. Reconstructions (contentious) of elements from villas at Rudston and Brantingham.

Jewry Wall Museum of Archaeology, St Nicholas Circle, Leicester. Telephone: Leicester (0533) 554100 extension 217. Meticulous reconstructions of wall decorations from suburban villa in Norfolk Street; much less reliable reconstructions from a house in Blue Boar Lane.

Leeds City Museum, Calverley Street, Leeds, West Yorkshire LS1 3AA. Telephone: Leeds (0532) 462632. Reconstructions, including part of ceiling, from bath house of villa at Dalton Parlours.

Lullingstone Roman Villa, Eynsford, Dartford, Kent. Telephone: Dartford (0322) 863467. Badly preserved painting of nymphs in position in a niche in the Deep Room.

Museum of London, London Wall, London EC2Y 5HN. Telephone: 01-600 3699. A few small fragments, including bird and flowers.

Museum of the Wiltshire Archaeological and Natural History Society, 41 Long Street, Devizes, Wiltshire SN10 1NS. Fragments, including head of a Cupid (?), from the villa at Box.

Roman Painted House, New Street, Dover, Kent CT17 9AJ. Telephone: Dover (0304) 203279. Lower parts of wall decorations in position in three rooms.

Scunthorpe Borough Museum and Art Gallery, Oswald Road, Scunthorpe, South Humberside DN15 7BD. Telephone: Scunthorpe (0724) 843533. Reconstruction (contentious) of figure painting from the bath house of the villa at Winterton.

Southwell Minster, Southwell, Nottinghamshire. Reconstruction (contentious) of figure painting, including Cupid, on display in south aisle; further pieces in store.

Verulamium Museum, St Michael's, St Albans, Hertfordshire AL3 4SW. Telephone: St Albans (0727) 54659, 59919 or 66100. Reconstructed decorations from various houses, including the 'barley stalk' ceiling; much further material in store, including reconstructed piece of ceiling plaster from villa at Gadebridge.

Viroconium Museum and Roman Site, Wroxeter, Shrewsbury, Shropshire. Telephone: Cross Houses (074 375) 330. Roman baths and site museum. Reconstructed piece of vault decoration from the hot room.

Winchester City Museum, The Square, Winchester, Hampshire SO23 9ES. Telephone: Winchester (0962) 68166 extension 269.

Reconstructed fragments from the city and from the villa at Sparsholt.

York Minster (Undercroft), York YO1 2HG. Reconstruction (contentious) of wall decoration from the headquarters building of the fortress.

Yorkshire Museum, Museum Gardens, York YO1 2DR. Telephone: York (0904) 29745. Areas of reconstructed wall decoration from Catterick.

Glossary

Arabesque: fanciful decorative motif in the form of spiralling or intertwining tendrils.

Burin: pointed implement used by engravers.

Candelabrum: vertical decorative element in wall-painting, loosely inspired by Roman lamp-stands; sometimes incorporating floral and vegetal motifs.

Chevron: V-shaped motif.

Chi-rho: Christian symbol formed from the initial letters (in Greek) of Christ's name.

Coffer: recessed panel in a ceiling or vault.

Corinthian capital: bell-shaped column-capital carved with acanthus leaves.

Cornice: projecting moulding in the upper part of a wall-decoration.

Dado: lowest zone in a wall-decoration.

Fascia: broad band.

Gorgon: mythical female whose look turned viewers to stone; her face, with snakes for hair, was a favourite decorative motif.

Lozenge: geometric figure in the form of a rhomboid.

Medallion: circular figure, roundel.

Nimbed: with a bright disc *(nimbus)* round the head.

Nymph: female spirit inhabiting woods, water etc.

Pilaster: pillar engaged in a wall.

Plasticity: the effect of having volume.

Podium: continuous projecting platform.

Predella: decorative frieze along the bottom of the main zone in a wall-decoration, especially popular in the Third Pompeian Style of painting.

Satyr: male spirit, one of the followers of the god Dionysus (Bacchus).

Socle: see *Dado.*

Stucco: fine white lime-plaster used in decorative relief.

Tesserae: cut stones or pieces of glass, generally cubic, used in mosaic (referred to, when undecorated, as *tessellation*).

Trompe l'oeil: form of painting designed to give so convincing an illusion of reality as to 'deceive the eye'; uses technical devices such as perspective, foreshortening and shading.

Index

Page numbers in italics refer to illustrations